BIRTH BY FIRE

A GUIDE TO HAWAII'S VOLCANOES

WRITTEN BY BOB KRAUSS • PHOTOGRAPHS BY G. BRAD LEWIS

TABLE OF

CONTENTS

Lava explodes into the Pacific Ocean at Kīlauea Volcano Park - Puna, Hawai‘i.

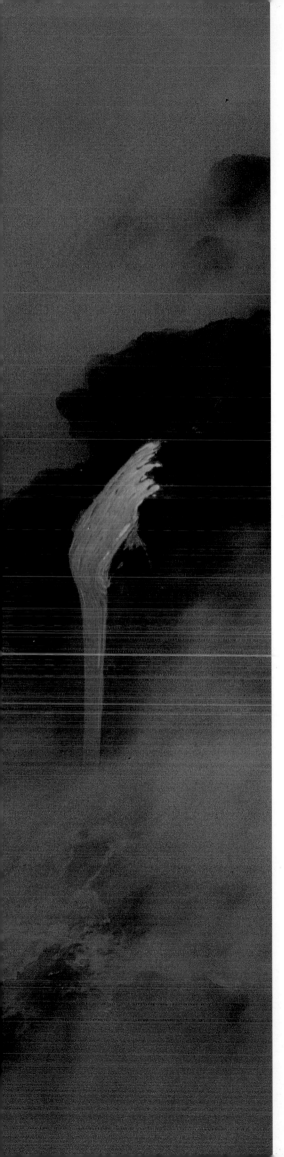

Acknowledgements

I would like to thank the people who have made the writing of this book an exciting experience for me. The staff of the Hawai'i Volcanoes National Park has been particularly helpful. The park's late supervisory park ranger, Jon Erickson, encouraged me, edited the manuscript and pointed out errors. Kathleen English, who is based at the park as executive director of the Hawai'i Natural History Association, read the manuscript and made helpful suggestions.

May I express my thanks for delightful and informative interviews with Laura Carter, Linda Cuddihy and Larry Katahira, all of the park staff, as well as with Reggie Okamura at the Hawai'i Volcano Observatory. Others who shared with me their knowledge of and love for the volcano are Kathy and Aku Hauanio, Pualani Kanakaole Kanahele, John Campbell, John Orr, Harry Kim and my old friend Gordon Morse. To my colleague, G. Brad Lewis, I owe thanks for his respect for the land as well as for his talent.

Bob Krauss

Bob Krauss

Lava flowing into the Pacific Ocean - Kalapana, Hawai'i.

Preface

You are about to embark upon a magnificent adventure, an expedition into the mysteries of nature's powerful force, the volcano. This guide is about how to make the most of an experience that can change the way you feel about the planet on which you live. Volcanoes have done this for humans for thousands of years.

With this guide, you can begin your volcano adventure anywhere in Hawai'i because each island is a volcano, or several. The volcano is all around you if you know how to look. But most of the following pages are about the legendary home of the fire goddess Pele with its internationally recognized scientific laboratory in the study of volcanoes on the Big Island of Hawai'i at Hawai'i Volcanoes National Park.

A journey to this center of elemental force can enlarge the mind, the senses and the spirit because a volcano is not just an eruption of molten rock. It is the miracle of creation, the regeneration that follows destruction, the response of humans to overpowering forces of nature, the evolution of plants and animals found nowhere else in the world, and the marvelously complex mythology that links all of these things together.

This book is about how to recognize and understand such fascinating surprises when they pop up around you in volcano country. Use the index to find what interests you most.

Kīlauea Volcano Lava Tube - Puna, Hawai'i.

New Horizon.

CHAPTER ONE

CREATION

Birth of a Volcano

In the beginning the earth trembles. But humans usually do not notice. The rising of magma (underground lava) in subterranean channels is like a subway locomotive that rumbles beneath a city, while citizens go about their business unaware of the vibration. Only sensitive instruments called seismographs record earth's impending decision to renew itself.

Even the most sophisticated scientists cannot predict exactly where this trembling will take place, on the summit of the volcano or along the rift zones on its flank. During historic times in Hawai'i, volcanic activity occurred most often in the crater of Kīlauea, home of the fire goddess Pele, and on the frigid heights of towering Mauna Loa volcano. But it has also happened within the last 40 years in a roadside cucumber patch, in a field of sugar cane beside a Hawaiian village, in numerous old volcano craters and in a remote tropical rain forest.

This unpredictable miracle begins when a fissure in the earth, sometimes miles long, opens. Magma from the mantle emerges, becoming lava on the surface. A curtain of fire pumps fountains of lava with indescribable energy. It is an assault on the senses. It is like standing in the door of a blast furnace. It is like enduring the screaming roar of a jet engine. You are breathing the gases of earth. And the glowing orange of lava is as shamelessly unreal as a picture postcard, flowing like a gaudy river of fire down the path of least resistance.

The volcano may pulsate for a few hours and then stop. Or it may pump for days, or weeks, or months, or years. Its curtain of fire soon may consolidate into a central fountain, building a crater and/or a cone of lava and/or pumice or cinders that will take a name in the history of volcanoes: Pu'u Puai, Mauna Ulu, Pu'u 'Ō'ō, Kupaianaha. These are on the map. They have created volcano country.

Sometimes the single fountain becomes more boisterous than the curtain of fire. The fountain of Kīlauea Iki in 1959 rose almost 2000 feet in a majestic display of elemental force, spewing ash that transformed a lush rain forest into stark skeletons of dead trees. Yet the same fountain built a mound of ash, rising

Lava enters the Pacific Ocean - Puna, Hawai'i.

River of lava at Kīlauea Volcano - Puna, Hawaiʻi.

above the cemetery of trees, upon which sunlight shines like a parent smiling at a newborn child. The volcano symbolizes life in the midst of destruction.

At Hawai'i Volcanoes National Park, you can experience this dichotomy as you walk the Devastation Trail, wasteland slowly returning to greenness. It happens not only here. New plant life springs up on barren lava flows all over the island. You need only to look out of the window of your auto or tour bus. Many of the plants and birds that have evolved out of volcanic devastation in Hawai'i are found nowhere else on earth. In earth's evolution they are as exciting as a volcanic eruption because they represent survival. The adventure is to recognize them.

Lava from the central fountain, like water, runs downhill. Pu'u 'Ō'ō erupted in a trackless wilderness on the flank of Kīlauea in 1983, and the fiery fingers of lava burned their way down through rain forest, hidden from curious humans. But then the lava arrived at the back door of a new housing development. Newspaper headlines exploded as the eruption consumed the homes of newcomers who discovered what it means to live with a volcano.

Those who understood best were residents of the charming old village of Kalapana, Hawaiians whose ancestors were more familiar with the mythology of the fire goddess, Pele. The homes of Hawaiians, too, were destroyed as lava flowed to the sea, and that refuge of Hawaiiana is no more. Chapter Three is about the close relationship between the volcano and the people who have lived with Pele since birth.

It is when lava reaches the sea that fire and water meet in elemental confrontation: in billows of steam, in the birth of new beaches, and in the building of islands as the ocean yields to expanding earth. All this happens during an eruption you can sometimes see and feel and stand in awe of. And as you walk out on the new land, you can hear with every step on the cold lava the crunching echo of creation.

Methane gas burning - Kalapana, Hawai'i.

Birth of Islands

Twenty-one miles south of Hawai'i lies what may one day become the newest member of the island chain. But it boasts no swaying palms or golden beaches because it has not yet emerged from beneath the surface of the ocean. Its name is Loihi.

This baby volcano has already risen more than 13,000 feet above the sea floor, and its crater lies only 3180 feet below the surface of the ocean. The best estimates are that it could break the surface during the next tens of thousands of years. Scientists in a mini-submarine have studied this infant or undersea volcano with great interest.

This provides us with an excellent lesson in the accepted theory of how the Hawaiian Islands came to be. Geologists think that Loihi rests over the edge of a hot spot in the earth's mantle where magma rises to build Hawai'i's volcanic islands from the sea floor. Yet the Hawaiian archipelago stretches more than 1500 miles from tiny Ocean Island in the northwest to Hawai'i in the southeast. How did so many volcanoes stray so far from the hot spot?

The answer lies in plate tectonics. This theory of continental drift holds that the earth's crust is divided into 14 rigid plates that drift on a more fluid part of the earth's mantle. Largest of all the plates is the Pacific plate. For the past 70 million years it has drifted northwest, currently at a rate of one to two inches a year, the same rate that your fingernails grow.

So a volcanic island built over the hot spot gradually drifts away on the plate and another volcanic island begins to form over the hot spot. Only those volcanoes on islands nearest the hot spot have erupted during historic times. Also, those islands farthest from the hot spot are the oldest. The island of Hawai'i is the youngest to be inhabited and is still in eruption.

Now we come to the kind of volcano exploring you can do on any Hawaiian island. Hawai'i's volcanoes build islands by piling one lava flow upon another. An imaginative volcanologist described the Big Island of Hawai'i as a "giant pile of candle drippings." The other Hawaiian islands are no different. This is obvious and fascinating when, on any island, you look at a sea cliff eroded by waves, or a cut in a hillside dug for a highway.

Hot lava bubbling - Puna, Hawai'i.

Boiling lava at Kīlauea Volcano's Kupianaha Vent - Puna, Hawai'i.

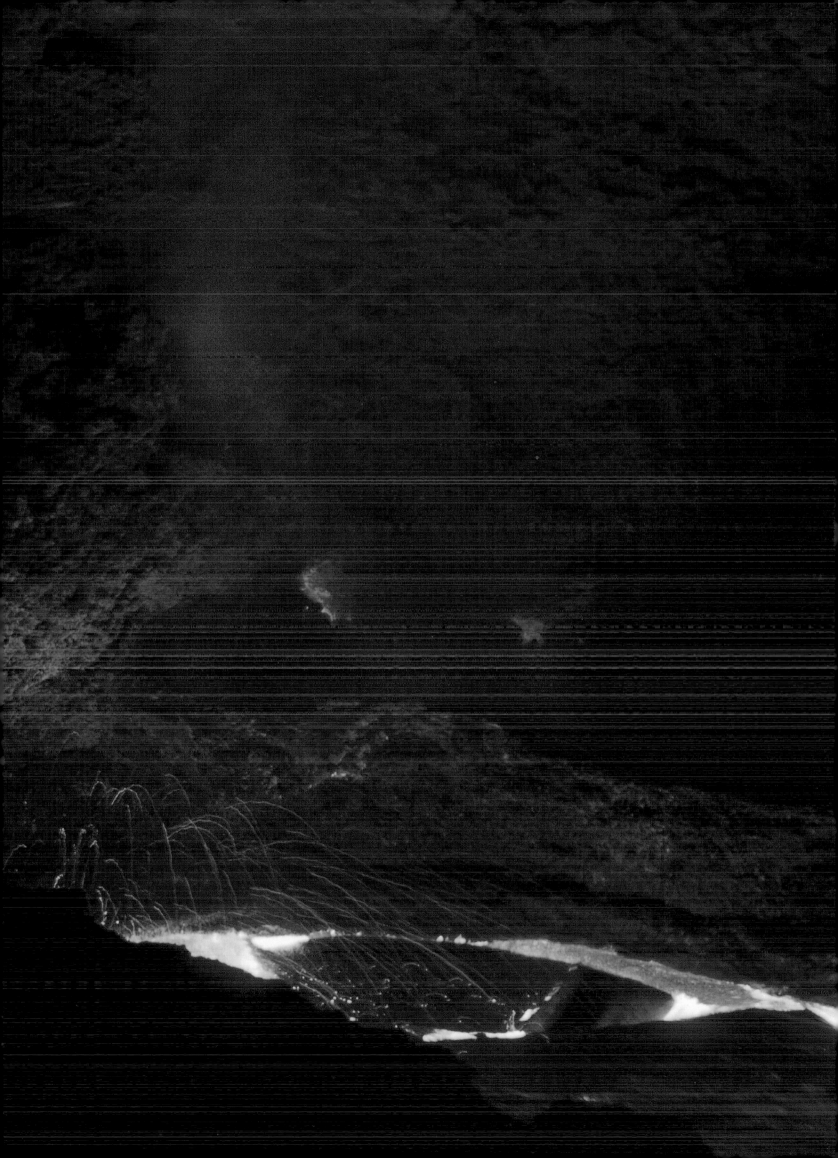

Lava pours into the ocean - Puna, Hawai'i.

There you may often see layer upon layer of lava that created the island. One layer might be ash while another might be rock, each from a different eruption.

Old craters all over the islands are more evidence of the volcanic genealogy of the Hawaiian Islands. Diamond Head, the famous landmark that anchors Waikīkī, is a crater formed during the death throes of a volcano. So is Punchbowl, home of the National Cemetery of the Pacific, in Honolulu. It is good sport to count as many craters as you can find while you travel about the islands.

Judging the age of a volcanic island is more difficult than recognizing craters. But it is not too different from judging the age of people, because you look for wrinkles. The great mounds of gently sloping lava that form Hawai'i's typical shield volcanoes on the Big Island are young and relatively smooth. Each island lying farther to the northwest is progressively older and more wrinkled, eroded by water and wind. So the volcanic mountains of O'ahu and Kaua'i, once smoothly sloping, have become towering buttresses of serrated cliffs. The romantic, jagged peaks of older islands result not from Pele's work but from the whimsy of wind and water.

Do not be confused by finding what appears to be more than one volcano on an island. All of Hawai'i's major islands were built by more than one volcano. (See Chapter Eight for more about the volcanoes of Maui, Kaua'i, O'ahu, Moloka'i and Lāna'i.)

The Big Island of Hawai'i required the services of no less than five different volcanoes in its massive construction, and you can see them all as you go exploring. There is Kohala forming the northwest tip, Hualalai to the west, the frequently snow-capped cone of Mauna Kea guarding the north, and huge Mauna Loa to the south with newer Kīlauea on its southwest flank.

No geologist cares to be pinned down as to the absolute age of these islands because they are too young to fit comfortably into the geologic timetable. A convenient method of dating rocks is by the fossils they contain. When you find fossils of dinosaurs you can be reasonably confident that you are dealing with the Mesozoic Era 65 to 225 million years ago. But many fossils found in Hawai'i's cliffs are from species so young they are still very much alive.

The only way to date Hawai'i's rocks is by less conventional methods such as chemical analysis. Even if such dates are accurate (and they probably are) they must seem somewhat meaningless to geologists to whom 100,000 years is a fleeting instant. In any case, one source estimates Kaua'i, the oldest major island, to be three to five million years old, and Hawai'i, the youngest, less than 700,000 years old.

So do not expect in Hawai'i to encounter the majestic sweep of time that you can read in the rocks of the Allegheny Mountains, created 230 million years ago, or the awesome timelessness of the Grand Canyon, where rocks on the canyon floor are two billion years old. The Colorado River began carving the Grand Canyon some six million years ago, perhaps before Kaua'i broke the surface of the ocean.

But if Hawaiian rocks do not possess the dignity of age, they make up for it with the excitement of youth. Where else can you walk on a piece of our planet that was created last year, or last week? Where else can you even, if you're lucky, watch the new land being created as lava flows into the sea?

Other coincidences make Hawai'i's volcanoes an opportunity for adventure like none other in the world. Most volcanoes around the globe erupt explosively, as did Mount Saint Helens in Washington State in 1980. In contrast, Hawai'i's volcanoes erupt gently. The height of a lava fountain depends not upon exploding gases, but upon the pressure forcing lava to the surface like water from a hose.

This benign reputation of Hawaiian volcanoes is due to their lavas. Hawaiian lavas have a lower content of the gases that cause explosions during volcanic eruptions elsewhere. Also, Hawaiian lavas are more fluid because they are hotter, up to 2200°F. Hotter lavas do not trap gases, but release them before they explode.

To complete your basic course in Hawaiian lava, you need only to recognize the two types whose names have been adopted around the world, *pāhoehoe* and *'a'a*. *Pāhoehoe* is hotter and flows like a river. A cooled *pāhoehoe* lava flow has a smooth, often shiny, billowy surface, rather like

chocolate pudding. *'A'a* creeps forward like a glacier. It is a huge mass of clinkers, volcanic slag, riding on molten stone. It advances like a giant worm, then cools to form a brutal surface of jagged, sharp-edged rock like a slag heap. Neither *pāhoehoe* nor *'a'a* in Hawai'i explode on eruption.

Lava explodes as it enters the Pacific Ocean.

Lava flow moving swiftly down the mountain: Kīlauea Volcano, Puna, Hawai'i.

This nonexplosive characteristic of Hawaiian volcanoes not only permits close scientific study (see Chapter Five, People Who Live With Volcanoes) but also allows visitors eyewitness views of eruptions, live lava flows, and the entry of lava into the sea to create new land.

Another fortunate coincidence is the remoteness of Hawai'i's volcanic islands. They are farther from a continental land mass than any other islands in the world. So all plants and animals found in Hawai'i needed, like yourself, to cross the ocean. Birds probably arrived on storm winds from the North American continent more than 2000 miles away. They carried stickery seeds on their feathers, in mud on their feet, or in their digestive systems to be evacuated on arrival. Spores might have traveled with the jet stream. Snails probably hitched rides on floating logs.

Bringing life to Hawai'i's barren volcanic islands in this way was a slow process. Not only was the journey hazardous, but a seed or a creature might find itself on arrival in an environment in which it could not live. Then it would die in spite of its heroic attempt at new settlement. This is why the fish of Hawaiian reefs are more closely related to those of Southeast Asia, which is 5000 to 7000 miles away, than to those of much closer California. Hawaiian waters are warmer than those in California, but similar in temperature to the oceans of Southeast Asia.

The establishment of each new life form in Hawai'i, before the arrival of humans, is estimated to have occurred at intervals of tens of thousands of years or more, each success a tribute to both luck and tenacity. What happened next is even more fascinating. In these remote islands, species proliferated that are found no-

Lava flowing into ocean, Hawai'i Volcanoes National Park.

where else on earth. The untold number of endemic species that evolved in Hawai'i make those found by Charles Darwin on the Galapagos Islands seem sparse.

Nowhere can you better explore this incredible miracle of evolution than in the national parks established in Hawai'i's volcano country: Haleakalā National Park on the island of Maui and the Hawai'i Volcanoes National Park on the island of Hawai'i. Here rare species of plants and birds still exist, species that park personnel are studying with the goal of preserving them. (See Chapter Four, Volcano Country, and Chapter Seven, How To Explore The Volcano.)

The parks are the heart of your volcano adventure, multidimensional lessons in relating to your planet. They are living examples of Genesis, the first chapter, a glimpse into the beginning of things.

Creation and Destruction

Volcano country is a land of profound irony.

You may walk for miles in philosophic contemplation over an expanse as barren as the surface of the moon. In fact, astronauts came to volcano country before the first moon shot to acclimate themselves.

But if there is no life on new lava, there is a spiritual energy, a lively spur to the imagination. The whorls, shapes and forms in the cold stone are both graceful and contorted, artistic and crude. They are a photographer's paradise. (For how to photograph lava and eruptions, see Chapter Five, People Who Live With Volcanoes.) Most of all they stimulate our inner being in response to desolation, the extinction of life, destruction by fire.

Yet the trail leads abruptly into the beauty of a tropical rain forest (Wao Kele O Puna). Here is exuberant life: sun-dappled, green and fresh, sweetened by the musical songs of rare bird species. This tropical rain forest, the only one in the United States, is both lovely and fragile. Populated by rare plants, it is a biological Garden of Eden. (See Chapter Four, Volcano Country, and Chapter Seven, How To Explore The Volcano.)

Eruptions rage through this sophisticated community of life, leaving a ruin of smoking desolation. What does this mean in human terms? What is the sense in it?

One answer may be in the tiny green flags of sword ferns and lichen and 'ohi'a that take root in a year or two on the raw lava to defy death in regeneration of the new land. Devastated sections of tropical rain forest, apparently destroyed, begin to grow again. Heavy rainfall in this part of volcano country makes them start to regenerate quickly. Artists, especially, seem inspired by such elemental energy in this unique form.

It is as if the volcano teaches us that creation and destruction are linked in the close embrace of birth and death, that desolation is the back side of hope, that the end is only the beginning. The volcano is a profound comment on our human situation, a spiritual place, and no people knew it better than the old Hawaiians.

VOLCANO MYTHOLOGY

Ancient Mythology of Pele

Pele is the only one of the old Hawaiian gods and goddesses whose name is today a household word, but in ancient times she was not a major or national deity. Those gods, for whom *kapu* or holy days of the month were observed, were Kū, Lono, Kāne and Kanaloa. Pele is by contrast an *'aumakua,* a lesser or family god.

Pualani Kanakaole Kanahele, an authority on Pele and Hawaiian tradition, is a person to whom park authorities go when they need advice about Hawaiiana. Pua, as she is called, is a dignified and intelligent Hawaiian woman whose ancestry is in the districts of Ka'ū and Puna, volcano country, the domain of Pele.

She explained that the ancient Hawaiians built *heiau* or temples for the worship of Kū, god of war, and Lono, god of peace and agriculture. She said the *kāhuna* or priests of such *heiau* had to be of the *ali'i,* or chiefly rank. *'Aumākua,* or family gods, were worshipped in less formal ways, and each family observed and passed down its own traditions of worship. Therefore, there is

Left, *Lava sculpture surrounded by hot lava.*

Right, *Pualani Kanahele.*

no universal ritual for the worship of Pele, an 'aumakua.

Asked to describe the ritual of her family, Pua said firmly, "It is not my responsibility to reveal the bones of my ancestors. It is my responsibility to guard them." She refused say whether or not she worships Pele, but was willing to describe the goddess as she understands her.

Pua said Pele can be approached on many levels. She can be discussed on a philosophical, intellectual level. She can

The Ray Fonseca Hālau.

be approached artistically through chants and the hula. She and her siblings can be recognized in lava, steam and regenerative vegetation. The worship of Pele as an ancestral goddess is another level.

"Pele is a woman of the east," said Pua. "The old *kāhuna* used to talk about Pele in terms of regeneration: a new day, the rising sun, the northeast trade winds, rain from the east.

"The primary function of Pele is creative. Destruction comes in the minds of humans relative to the things being destroyed...If she has to take Queen's Bath (a popular scenic playground covered by a recent flow) to create, she does. We get used to seeing these beautiful things so we call Pele a destructive force. Until beautiful things start to grow (again) and start to live."

Another reason for Pele's survival may be that she is among the most colorful of the gods in the Hawaiian pantheon. The legends of Pele tell about her search for a home, moving down the chain of islands from Kaua'i, digging her fire pits but always striking water until she came at last to the crater of Kīlauea where she remains. Pele's route of island hopping, from the oldest volcanoes to the newest, indicates that the old Hawaiians understood volcano science with considerable sophistication.

But the goddess is not only a keeper of volcanoes. She is a tempestuous and jealous lover who flies into rages. She is also beautiful. Her sisters, Laka and Hi'iaka, are the artistic patrons of the hula. Pua is a *kumu hula,* or hula master, and her *hālau* (school) performs dances to Pele that Pua described as "very bombastic, low to the ground, connected to the earth." Pele's brothers include a shark god, a god of explosions, a fire maker and a god of thunder.

26

Modern Volcano Folklore

Missionary William Ellis in 1823 was the first western visitor who was warned not to take things that belong to Pele. He was walking around the island looking for places to establish Congregational churches when he picked some *'ōhelo* berries, an endemic fruit, at the volcano. His Hawaiian guides, aghast, immediately stopped him and instructed him in the ritual. (For the proper way to pick *'ōhelo* berries, and how to distinguish them from poisonous berries, see Chapter Five, People Who Live With Volcanoes.)

The modern folklore of Pele also teaches the old Hawaiian practice of cooperation as a survival technique. People on remote islands depend on one another. Hospitality is more than good manners: it is necessary, and reciprocity is expected.

Shortly after I arrived in Hawai'i in the early 1950s, I was shown Pele's domain by the late Richard Lyman, a respected *kama'āina* (native) of Puna, the backyard of Pele. You may follow the same route today over smoothly paved roads that were then bumpy, narrow gravel.

Lyman promised to show me petrified Hawaiians. I could not tell from his sober, Hawaiian-Abraham-Lincoln face whether or not he was pulling my leg. Yet I became more and more curious as we drove through a mysterious tropical forest where mist hung heavy as on the moor of the Baskervilles. Lyman stopped the car and pointed to painfully contorted shapes formed in stone, lonely and timeless in the mist. The back of my neck prickled.

"There are the petrified Hawaiians," said Lyman. "They lived here in a village where Pele asked for food. The villagers refused to share with her. She went away but, to teach the selfish villagers a lesson, Pele sent a lava flow that turned them into stone." An ancient Hawaiian legend from the same locality makes a similar point.

Lava Tree State Park - Puna, Hawai'i.

The place that Lyman showed me as a part of his Puna heritage is now called Lava Tree Park, a lovely spot preserved by the state. There is no better place to view tree stumps engulfed in lava to create anthropomorphic shapes. (For more on lava trees, see Chapter Seven, How to Explore the Volcano.) Lyman's eyes twinkled as he told the story. Yet he always bridled when *haoles* (foreigners or whites) chided him about his deep respect for Hawaiian traditions, especially those regarding Pele.

Pele's power to put to death people who did not observe the Hawaiian practice of hospitality and respect for herself apparently diminished over the years. In the 1950s, as a newspaper columnist, I received several reports from people of various islands who said they stopped to pick up an old woman by the side of the road. They said she got into the back seat, then asked for a cigarette. On offering her one, the driver smelled the sulphur of a wooden match as she lit up. Later, he looked back to find the back seat empty. Then he realized that his passenger had been Pele and he was glad that he had stopped to give her a ride. For, if he hadn't, he would have bad luck. In ancient times, he would have died. I wrote these stories and was always interested in their cultural context.

Even today, when *The Honolulu Advertiser* publishes a photo of steam rising from an eruption, or of a lava fountain, readers frequently call in to point out Pele's face in the photograph.

Above, *Ferns, Haleakalā Crater, Maui.*

Right, *Gin offering to Pele - Kalapana, Hawai'i.*

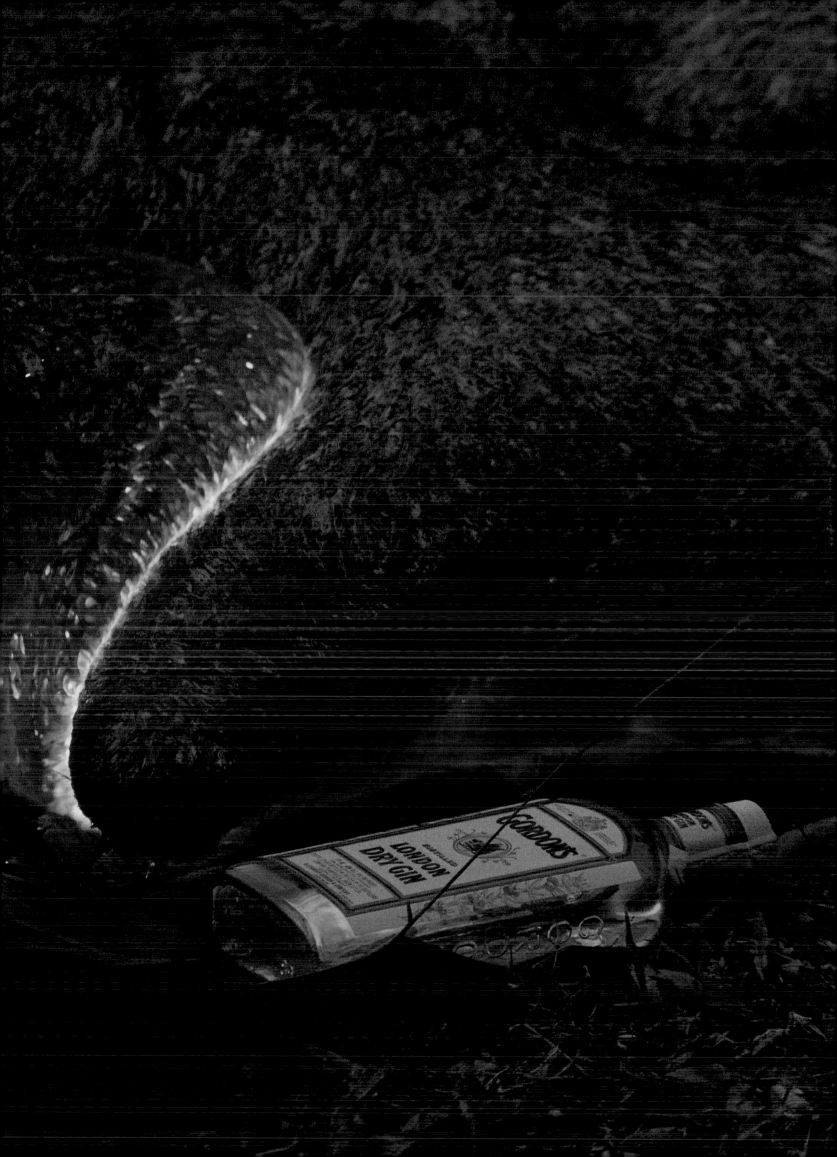

CHAPTER THREE

THE LONG ERUPTION

"The volcano put us on alert at 12:30 A.M. on January 2, 1983, when the tremor alarm tripped, indicating movement of molten rock underground," said Jon Erickson, who was superintendent of the Hawai'i Volcanoes National Park until his death in late 1991. "We all raced to the observatory to see what the instruments were telling us.

"By two o'clock, four of us were perched on the slope of Mauna Ulu anticipating an outbreak which did not occur, but instead migrated underground six miles to erupt in Nāpau Crater and beyond. One of the vents opened up in a place identified on the topographical map as 'lava flow of 1965.' The vent opened up on the letter 'O.' That's why we identified it as the O Vent."

So began what has become the longest eruption in recorded history on Kīlauea's east rift, and by far the most destructive in human terms. New land and new beaches have been created in profusion. Visitors from around the world have thronged to see the lava flow into the sea, and photographs have appeared in publications in many languages.

But the eruption at first eluded people eager to see the outbreak because it occurred in a rain forest far above the seacoast village of Kalapana. The fountain rose in a place so remote that no roads led there. Tours by helicopter boomed.

As usual, the lava fountain subsided, then pulsed again; and the fire consumed only rain forest. But this time the eruption was not to be a mere sideshow for humans.

By March 1983, two houses had burned and civil defense officials were evacuating subdivisions. In the years that followed, two dramas were played out in this back yard of Pele. One was headlined in the newspapers, the other quietly conducted by archaeologists headed by Laura Carter of the park staff. They worked tirelessly to excavate ancient sites on the seacoast, salvaging secrets about the people of old before the lava covered this priceless information.

Lava burns down a house in Kalapana, Hawai'i.

"We got incredible artifacts," said Carter, an outdoor woman of courage and scholarship in her profession. "We would arrive at our site early in the morning in the glow of the eruption. But I felt serene and tranquil. We were confronted on a daily basis by the lava flow. We were excavating while the lava advanced one hundred yards away.

"When lava crossed the trail, I had to walk over the flow to a site. It seemed that we were allowed just enough time to finish each site. The next morning it was covered by lava. I don't think of the sites as being destroyed. I think of them as being preserved, very well preserved, because we know where they are under the lava."

Meanwhile, flows advanced through the new subdivisions destroying 25 buildings, then 50, then 100 and, finally, nearly 200. For some reason, the lava did not cover Waha'ula Heiau, only embraced it. But Queen's Bath, a favorite picnic and bathing spot, is now beneath the lava.

The flows stopped and started again in Pele's capricious way until in 1990 they threatened the old village of Kalapana. Once more the flow stopped and the villagers read headlines that said, "Kalapana Gets Word, Crisis Over." But a week later, another outbreak of lava began to roll toward the charming old village. People frantically removed their possessions.

Members of Kalapana's historic Catholic church moved it just ahead of the advancing lava. Members of the community's Congregational church, after praying for guidance, packed away the Bibles, the crystal, a flagon presented by Princess Lili'uokalani and the church bell, and left their house of worship in the hands of God. It was consumed, and they now hold services in a new place.

A young Hawaiian family—Aku and Kathy Hauanio and their three children–described the trauma of losing their home to the lava. Aku said he and his brothers and sisters were born in his father's house next door. The whole family gathered to watch their birthplace go up in flames.

"My daddy planted fruit trees in his yard to feed the children before we were born," said Aku. "He had breadfruit, mango, avocados, coconuts. He cried that morning when the lava came in. He hasn't been back since. Our children miss the trees. They played in them. They miss the beach (buried under lava) because that was their playground."

Kathy and Aku said they thought their house would be safe from the lava because it was on a little rise and protected by two stone walls. They thought the walls would divert the lava. But the stone walls were like matchsticks braced to stop a flood. When the lava oozed over the walls, Aku and Kathy knew they had to get out. The lava came in incredible abundance, filling hollows 100 feet deep as if they were mud puddles.

Aku's aunties, uncles, cousins, in-laws and friends pitched in to help. A moving crew got their house away four hours ahead of the lava. Meanwhile, 25 people dug up the flowering plants in which the family took so much pride. Because soil is precious in lava country, they dug up the dirt they had trucked in for their vegetable garden.

A lava flow burns the forest near "Left Point" surf break - Kalapana, Hawai'i.

"We had cucumbers, eggplants, tomatoes, sweet potatoes, corn, beans and herbs," said Kathy. "Our best crop was the last. It was as if the land was trying to show what it could do before the lava came." The couple took away 300 coconuts from the old trees as a new source of life.

A friend invited the Hauanios to put their house on his land down the coast. They live there now, still awed by the force of nature that changed their lives. But neither Aku nor Kathy is bitter. "We don't believe in Pele," Aku said quietly. "Pele is just a name. The Lord gives and the Lord takes away. Lava is the masterpiece of the Lord."

Kathy said, "It's hard to be angry with creation, as much as it takes away. I wished it would stop. But you can't be resentful against nature."

In their new front yard on a slope overlooking the vast blue Pacific, the 300 coconuts they saved from their old home site are now sprouting bravely, the beginnings of a grove of tall, graceful palm trees. Here and there bits of color from blooming flowers testify to the new start Aku and Kathy have made. "I tell the children we have a piece of our property up here," said Aku.

Remember this when you walk over the barren desolation of new lava at Kalapana.

Residents of this area have long been familiar with the moods of the volcano. They have had a long time to learn. Archaeological evidence indicates that Hawaiians in the old days did not live permanently near Pele's mountain residence in Kīlauea Crater. They knew the area well from constant traveling about the island. But the homes of people who lived in Big Island volcano country were mostly scattered along the warmer seacoast in the districts of Puna and Ka'ū as shown on maps of the island.

So your volcano adventure also includes these districts where there are more opportunities for exploration, including old ruins. Puna and Ka'ū are as different as night and day for a basic reason. The northeast trade winds drop their rain on the northeast or windward sides of all the islands. The opposite or leeward sides receive less rain. That is why Puna, to windward, is a lush, tropical paradise while Ka'ū, to leeward, is known for its Ka'ū Desert.

Bone fishhooks and other artifacts found in archaeological digs at South Point on the parched and windy tip of Ka'ū indicate that the first settlers in Hawai'i came from the Marquesas Islands in the South Pacific, 2000 miles away, perhaps 1500 years ago or more. You can still see a small *heiau* of later vintage on the point near the lighthouse, and mooring holes chipped into the edge of the cliff where Hawaiians tied their canoes. Look where modern fishermen have built modern moorings.

The Marquesans were followed perhaps 500 or 1000 years later by the more sophisticated Tahitians, who brought new gods and established the chiefly system. One of these pioneers was a famous priest named Paau who came to Puna and built Waha'ula Heiau, possibly the oldest in the Islands, for the new god, Kū. Waha'ula Heiau, near the ocean on a lava coast, is inside

---

Fire hydrant entombed by lava, Harry K. Brown Park - Kalapana, Hawai'i.

Lava destroys a house - Kalapana, Hawaiʻi.

Hawai'i Volcanoes National Park. The venerable walls of this historic ruin at this writing stand surrounded by lava from a recent flow.

A little farther out toward the ocean you can find another Hawaiian ruin: a small, rude circular structure of stone that fishermen built as a windbreak. These are common all over this coast. Also along the way, off Chain of Craters Road, is a field of petroglyphs chipped into the *pāhoehoe* lava, stick figures and mysterious circles whose meaning passed away with the people who made them. Look for the sign along the road.

In tropical Puna, cooled by the trade winds, the Hawaiian pioneers came to know the volcano well, for flow after flow ravaged their new land. It was thus probably in Puna that the mythology of Pele evolved, perhaps before Paau and the new national gods arrived. Here descendants of the pioneers built their houses of *pili* grass or *lolou* palm fronds, fished in the sea, planted their crops of dry land taro and sweet potatoes, pounded *wauke* or mulberry bark to make *kapa* for clothing, and worshipped the new gods.

Our first eyewitness report of this picturesque seacoast and its Hawaiian population came from the indefatigable William Ellis on his tour around the island in 1823. After a side trip to Kīlauea Crater, Ellis returned to the sea at a small fishing village in dry Ka'ū named Kealakomo. He followed the lava-bound coast past the village of Kamoamoa (see your map), where you will now find a new black sand beach and a picnic ground and many *noni* apples, a fruit used for medicinal purposes by the people of old.

Ellis walked beyond ancient Waha'ula Heiau into increasingly lush vegetation as he entered Puna. At Kalapana Village

House destroyed by lava at Kalapana Gardens subdivision, Kalapana, Hawai'i.

he reported a population of 2000. (At this writing, travelers can no longer continue on to Kalapana because lava blocks the road.) Farther on, the plantations of the Hawaiians became richer and more numerous, and the scenery spectacular. At 'Opihikao, Ellis preached the blessings of Jehovah.

Lava flowing down the road.

Today you will find there, under the coconut palms, a prim New England church that traces its lineage back to that first sermon on the shore.

The road, a marvelous adventure through the jungle, continues on to the craters of Kapoho, where the natives told Ellis about the volcanic origin of their land. Infuriated by this invasion of Pele's domain by the new God, a priestess of Pele vowed vengeance upon the missionaries. But the power of the fire goddess was on the wane. A high chieftess named Kapi'olani, a convert to Christianity, traveled in 1825 to Kīlauea Crater where, in an act of unbelievable courage, she spit upon Pele and defied her. The new God proved superior.

Mysterious Puna lay in tropical beauty, an isolated backwash of Hawaiiana, into the middle of the 20th century. Progressive Hawaiian land-owners such as Richard Lyman preached the fruitfulness of Puna. Here would grow papayas, anthuriums, vegetables, *kalo* (taro). The land waited to be productive. And Puna slowly stirred as papaya growers, using modern techniques, proved its agricultural potential. Cheap land invited real estate speculators who laid out subdivisions.

But the old village of Kalapana that William Ellis knew remained a Hawaiian place, home for families who had dealt with Pele for generations. There were two churches in the village, Catholic and Congregational. In the little frame Catholic church, an artistically inclined priest long ago used house paint to depict the saints on the inside walls. And so the Painted Church became a tourist attraction, as did the lovely black sand beach nearby.

The people and the church have been relocated, and the site is now buried beneath billows of black lava. Yet life in Puna goes on in the shadow of the volcano because, to people like Kathy and Aku Hauanio, this is home.

CHAPTER FOUR

WHAT TO LOOK FOR IN VOLCANO COUNTRY

This chapter describes in greater detail some of the many adventures awaiting you in volcano country, and how to recognize and appreciate them. For people who want to dig deeper, we will list books about different subjects that can take you beyond this introductory guide, either as beginners or graduates. Now let's go exploring in Big Island volcano country.

Mauna Kea and Mauna Loa

Two magnificent volcanoes dominate the skyline from the rim of Kīlauea Crater in Hawai'i Volcanoes National Park. The nearer one is Mauna Loa (Long Mountain) and the one in the distance is Mauna Kea (White Mountain).

They are two of the largest mountains in the world, rising more than 13,000 feet from sea level and over 30,000 feet from the ocean bottom. Mauna Kea is probably the highest mountain in the world when measured from base to summit. Mauna Loa is considered to be the largest single mountain mass in the world.

The eruptions of Mauna Loa have not only created half of the island but have shaped its history. In 1926, lava flowed from the southwest rift of Mauna Loa and buried the village of Ho'ōpūloa. In 1942, four months after Pearl

One of the many observatories atop Mauna Kea, Hawai'i.

Mauna Kea, Hawai'i.

Harbor was bombed, a summit-flank eruption of Mauna Loa intensely embarrassed military leaders in Hawai'i during the most tense days of World War II. The Hawaiian Islands were under a complete blackout. But the eruption could be seen from O'ahu. Tokyo Rose complimented Hawai'i on its fine volcanic eruption.

In 1984 an eruption broke out on the summit of Mauna Loa, sending nearly two million cubic yards of lava an hour in the direction of Hilo, covering nine miles the first day. Concern mounted in the city, and some residents began packing their belongings. By March 29, the flow had advanced to within five miles of Hilo when it slowed and finally stopped.

The threat of lava flows from the crater of Moku'āweoweo and from the flanks of the enormous mountain may affect the future of the Big Island. At least, government planners have begun to consider such potential eruptions. They are concerned about the safety of the Ka'ū coast, where developers are hoping to build resorts.

The Mauna Loa Strip Road will take you up the mountain to about 6600 feet. A foot trail continues from there. A road up Mauna Kea reaches the top, where an international settlement of observatories scan the skies. The astronomers live at about 9000 feet.

Two easy-to-read books for beginners about the geological aspects of these and Hawai'i's other volcanoes are *Volcanoes of the National Park of Hawai'i* by Gordon A. Macdonald and Douglass H. Hubbard, and *Volcano Watching* by Robert and Barbara Decker. The book for graduate geologists is *Volcanoes in the Sea* by Gordon A. Macdonald, Agatin T. Abbott and Frank L. Peterson.

Lava Tubes

Lava tubes are one reason that lava from an eruption high on the flank of Mauna Loa or Kīlauea reaches the sea many miles away. Lava tubes form when the outer surface of the flow cools and crusts over. This outer crust becomes a conduit for molten rock on the inside. The lava tubes thus created are sometimes many miles long. When the eruption ceases and lava drains out, the tube becomes a subterranean cavern with a roughly domed roof and a flat floor.

Early Hawaiians found these caverns to be convenient temporary housing and used them for camp sites after they built houses. A small lava tube near the sea in the Honolulu suburb of Kuli'ou'ou in 1951 produced the first carbon date in all of Polynesia and started a revolution in dirt archaeology in the Pacific.

The Hawaiians used other lava tubes as wartime refuges and as burial sites. The locations of burial caves of chiefs, and of families, were kept secret because bones were believed to contain *mana* or spiritual power, and valuable objects might be buried with the dead. Puna, with its long history of eruptions, has some of the most impressive lava tubes in the Hawaiian Islands. Several were discovered only recently to contain artifacts and stonework left there by the people of old. Steps have been taken to protect them from damage.

Probably the most famous lava tube in the Hawaiian Islands, the Thurston Lava Tube, is in the Hawai'i Volcanoes National Park. To walk a short section of that dim cavern is to understand the vastness of a major lava tube and the plumbing of a volcano.

Tropical Rain Forest

Volcano country is rich in one-of-a-kind plants. Finding them is an adventure you can't have elsewhere. Linda Cuddihy, biological technician at the park and an expert on Hawai'i's tropical rain forest, is your tour guide for this quick introduction.

"A tropical rain forest is a closed canopy forest often distinguished by a high diversity of plant species that get about 100 or more inches a year of rain," she said. "Most people don't even know there is a tropical rain forest in the United States."

This forest of tropical Hawai'i is different from the great tropical rain forests of the Amazon, Africa or Asia. One reason is that Hawai'i's tropical rain forest developed in isolation. As a result, numerous species growing

The Wao Kele O Puna tropical rain forest.

there are endemic, found nowhere else in the world. Also, many exotic or foreign species never reached Hawai'i, so the forest here is less complicated. The two major canopy trees are:

'Ohi'a—This endemic tree is a signature of the volcano, a marvelously gnarled character with a gray, shaggy bark and a crimson, pompon blossom. Cuddihy said the Hawaiian belief that picking an *'ohi'a* blossom will make it rain is "a pretty good bet because it rains so much up here." The *'ohi'a* provides Hawaiian lei makers with greenery. You see the hardy *'ohi'a* at sea level as well as in the mountains, and it is one of the first plants that takes root in a new lava flow.

Koa—The *koa* grew to giant size in olden days with towering trunks and spreading limbs. Hawaiians carved golden *koa* canoes from logs 60 or more feet long. The tree has a small, silvery, crescent-shaped leaf. Because *koa* furniture is in such demand, *koa* trees have been cut to near extinction. Cuddihy advised that the best place to view *koa* is on the Mauna Loa Strip Road at about 7000 feet in open grass land.

Two other plants that make volcano country unique are:

Ferns—The giant tree ferns you see on your way to the Thurston Lava Tube sometimes grow 30 feet tall. There are about 100 fern species in the park, three of which are found only in Hawai'i. The sword fern is one of the first plants to regenerate in a new lava flow. Ferns are a favorite material for Hawaiian lei makers.

'Ōhelo—This unique plant, familiar in volcano folklore, is a shrub found on open lava around Kīlauea Crater. It grows no more than three or four feet high, usually smaller, with a small-toothed leaf. Cuddihy said *'ōhelo* is related to the blueberry. The color of the berries varies from orange to red to yellow. (For the proper way to pick *'ōhelo* berries and how to recognize poisonous berries, see the next chapter.)

A collection of young hapu'u ferns.

As a book for beginning botanists, Cuddihy recommended *Trailside Plants of Hawai'i's National Parks* by Charles H. Lamoureux. She said graduates may prefer *A Manual of the Flowering Plants of Hawai'i* in two volumes by Warren L. Wagner, Derral R. Herbst and S. H. Sohmer.

Birds at the Volcano

Like the plants of volcano country, its birds excite some people more than eruptions do. Larry Katahira, resource management specialist at Hawai'i Volcanoes National Park, had windows cut into the walls of his office so he could look out and see the *'amakihi* and the *'apapane* flit from tree to tree. These birds, both types of honeycreepers, are common in the park but found nowhere else in the world. So Katahira will be your bird watching guide for this introductory tour.

He said that Kipuka Puaulu Bird Park is not the best place for bird watching. Drive instead to the upper portion of the Mauna Loa Strip Road. Below are listed the birds, unique to Hawai'i unless otherwise specified, that he suggests you look for:

'Apapane—If you see a flash of red exploding out of an *'ohi'a* tree before 9 A.M., the chances are it's an *'apapane* having breakfast. Its bill is slightly curved and black. *'Apapane* forages in the forest. Its call is a loud, upslurred whistle and its wings make a whirring sound in flight.

'Amakihi—This character is so exclusive there are separate species for each island. Males are yellowish green and dress in brighter colors than the drab females. One of the most common of endemic forest birds, its call is a buzzy tweet.

'Elepaio—Hawai'i *'elepaio* are brown and chestnut with bold markings in white and black. The call of this flycatcher is a squeaky chup-chup and its song a loudly whistled "el-e-pai-o." This bird eats insects on the fly or from tree bark.

'I'iwi—Adults are bright vermilion with long, curved, salmon-colored bills. One call is a distinct, clear whistle; another is an unmusical squeak. Look high in *'ohi'a* trees. The *'i'iwi*, another type of honeycreeper, appears in ancient chants because its red feathers were plucked to make the cloaks of sacred chiefs.

Nēnē—This is a handsome descendant of a Canadian goose who got lost and ended up in Hawai'i to become the state bird. Found only in Hawai'i and recently nearly extinct, the *nēnē* is fighting back. The body is heavily barred gray-brown, head black, neck buff and furrowed. Drive slowly in the park and *nēnē* will pose for your camera on the lava.

White-Tailed Tropicbird—Look for this lovely creature cavorting in craters. It nests in crater cliffs, but the parents fly all the way to the ocean to fish and bring back food for their young. The bird is poetry in motion on the wing, brilliant white with two long tail streamers. This bird is also found elsewhere in the Pacific.

The book about birds that Katahira recommended for beginners is *Hawai'i's Birds* published by the Hawai'i Audubon Society. For graduates he recommended *The Birds of Hawai'i & the Tropical Pacific* by H. Douglas Pratt, Phillip L. Bruner, and Delwyn G. Berrett.

Hawai'i's State bird, the Nēnē goose, as seen at Haleakalā National Park.

Friendly Advice

An internationally known bird watcher from England benefited from the help of Hawai'i's leading ornithologists who served as guides during his visit to volcano country. Yet he confessed he saw more endemic species in the driveway of his bed-and-breakfast before he sat down for pancakes in the morning than he did on formal bird walks. People who have lived in volcano country for years are still discovering new adventures in similar ways.

So you don't need expert advice to enjoy yourself. What you do need is an understanding that you are in the midst of a place unique on our planet, a place that offers multidimensional experiences through the sciences, religion, art and all the senses.

The next chapter tells how volcano country residents find the adventures you are looking for.

CHAPTER FIVE

PEOPLE WHO LIVE WITH VOLCANOES

There are special aspects of the volcano country that are best described by some of the people in charge of them. So let us turn in this chapter to the people who live with volcanoes to find out how you can share in the adventures they live every day.

Volcanology

Reggie Okamura, chief of operations at the Hawai'i Volcano Observatory

A staff of more than two dozen geologists, geophysicists, electricians, computer experts and electronics technicians monitor volcanic activity at the observatory located on the rim of Halema'uma'u Crater. Here is a scenic overlook and an excellent small museum that explains the work of scientists at the observatory.

Okamura has been a member of this select staff for more than 30 years. "This is a very desirable assignment," he said. "The observatory is a showcase for the U.S. Geological Survey. It has always been internationally known for the development of monitoring techniques and hazard mitigation type of work. I consider myself fortunate to be in a job I enjoy so much. Once you get rock fever you can't get over it.

"We still haven't learned what there is to know about volcanoes. Even with all the sophisticated instrumentation we've invented, we really haven't learned much about defining when a volcano will stop. We know more about predicting when it will start.

Samson Kaawaloa fishing next to lava flow - Kalapana, Hawai'i.

"The most exciting part of an eruption is the onset. It builds up with triggering mechanisms—quakes recorded on our instruments, inflation of the mountain that shows on our tilt meters. It's always exciting at that time, no matter how many eruptions you've been through. Kīlauea Iki was the most exciting for me because it was my first. While the fountaining rose to 2000 feet, the whole observatory building shook from the vibration."

Okamura downplayed the considerable danger of his job. Volcanologists walk over newly crusted lava flows to take their measurements. Once, when Okamura was drilling to take the temperature of the lava below, superheated steam shot from the hole and burned his leg. Another time, the wind shifted while he worked under a lava fountain. Hot pumice fell around him and set fire to the forest across the trail. Okamura scrambled to safety up the wall of an old crater. "The mystery of a volcano always intrigues me," he said. "There are so many unanswered questions."

Volcano Art and Photography

Boone Morrison, architect and founder of the Volcano Art Center
G. Brad Lewis, volcano photographer who lives in Puna

The Volcano Art Center is located within the Hawai'i Volcanoes National Park. It displays the work of local artists and is one of the best places in the state to see and buy Hawaiian handicrafts and art of quality. Founder Morrison explained why volcano country has become a magnet for artists of international reputation:

"Creative human spirits tend to gather in certain places on the planet; the Hudson River Valley in early America, Carmel after World War I, Taos, New Mexico. Psychic energy draws people to these places. Hawaiians call it *pūnāwai,* the well spring or source. There is vibrant energy at the volcano of a place that is alive. The dynamism is natural, and it has not been spoiled or commercialized. Artists here feel comfortable. This is a place to be in tune with the planet."

He said artists of every discipline live at the volcano: architects, musicians, poets, dancers, painters, woodworkers, photographers and many potters. "After all, Pele is the ultimate potter," Morrison explained.

Freelance photographer Lewis is noted for his poetic images of the volcano. His photos appear in major magazines in the United States and Europe, including *Life* and *Time*, and in this book. Here is his advice about how to photograph the volcano and why he does it:

"The best time to shoot the volcano is in early morning and late in the day, the transition times. I call it the magic hour. The same is true for an eruption and for cold lava. Lava is a tricky thing to shoot because it's so reflective. A lot of it is like glass. Midday light washes it out.

"As a photographer, I am fascinated by the texture and light of a volcano. It's something found nowhere else on the planet, and this eruption is so gentle that you get a chance to interact with it, a chance to walk up to these amazingly

G. Brad Lewis, volcano photographer.

beautiful and powerful things. My favorite thing to do is to catch the lava flowing into the ocean at dawn between light at dark. There's something very dynamic going on.

"I started out taking photographs of cold lava. The texture of it fascinates me. It's so dynamic to observe what was happening when it froze to solid rock. To me lava is raw nature, like earth blood. It's exciting."

Volcano Chasing

Gordon Morse, proprietor of a bed-and-breakfast near the park

Most volcano chasers begin as either newsmen or photographers. Morse began his career as a reporter in Honolulu, bouncing off to eruptions the way a fireman answers the alarm. Then he retired to volcano country, where he has become an amateur authority on the volcano. He picks *'ōhelo* berries, walks the trails, watches birds and instructs his guests in how to view an eruption safely with maximum enjoyment.

"The first eruption is the most exciting for everyone," he said. "I tell my guests to go in the evening before it gets dark, and I give them flashlights. The next morning at breakfast, you never heard such a hubbub. Everybody is telling everybody else what they saw and what it means to them. People send me photographs from all over the world.

"I pick *'ōhelo* berries to make sauce for my pancakes. The Hawaiians told William Ellis how to pick *'ōhelo* berries, and you'd better do it right. You take some, face toward the crater and say, 'Pele, I have picked your *'ōhelos*. These I give to you.' You toss them in the direction of the crater. Then you say, 'And now I will pick some for myself.'"

Morse advises volcano visitors about how to distinguish *'ōhelo* berries from inedible berries growing in the park, one species of which was used as a narcotic fish poison. The *'ōhelo* is like a blueberry with a soft skin and a pulpy interior. Its color ranges through pink, red and yellow. Inedible berries are smaller, with tough skins and hard interiors. *'Ōhelo* bushes are scraggly, with berries often outnumbering the leaves; inedible berries grow on more luxuriant bushes.

Morse has one more piece of advice for visitors: "Nobody has seen the park unless they have walked the trails. I thought I had seen them all until the seasons changed. Then they were different. What saddens me is people who race around and miss so much. There is no other place like this in the world. You'd better take a picture because eruptions keep changing the view. Your grandchildren probably won't see what you do."

Love of the Land

John Orr, 40-year resident of Puna

Orr and his late wife fell in love with the tropical mystery of Puna in the 1950s, leased a lot on a black lava shore and remained into their old age. They soon discovered the house they had built was on an ancient Hawaiian village. Canoe sheds, paved trails and other ancient stone ruins stood where they wanted to put such proper manifestations of suburban living as fences, a lawn and flower beds.

Orr did not remove the ruins. Instead, he spent years learning the history of Puna, researching the significance of those old Hawaiian obstacles to modern living. Today he is an authority on ancient Hawaiian trails. He has collected old maps of the area, and his interest in Hawaiian ruins has led to highly valued friendships with his Hawaiian neighbors. He is more proud of his ruins than he is of his house.

John Orr has preserved the heritage he inadvertently came to possess. He didn't destroy it. He is someone with the sensitivity to appreciate historic values, and to forgo development in favor of preservation so that his children may enjoy the pleasure he has found in the heritage of Puna. Hawaiians have a phrase for this. It is, "Love of the *aina* (land)."

John Orr, 40-year resident of Puna (left), with author Bob Krauss (right).

Attitudes of Government Officials

Harry Kim, Hawai'i County Civil Defense director

Kim is in charge of public safety on the Island of Hawai'i during eruptions. He is respected for his sensitivity to the grief of volcano victims during the destruction of Kalapana. Kim said that while spectators should be able to view the awesome phenomenon of an eruption, he also has to consider the safety of life and property. So he has kept spectators away from an eruption at times, and asked them not to violate the privacy of eruption victims.

Kim said he has to view an eruption as a force of nature that can change someone's entire way of life. He has to deal with the destructive force of a volcano that can hurt people and take away land. This has nothing to do with his respect for Pele, he added. He said the destruction of Kalapana taught him much as a government official:

"I remember talking to a person who was losing his land and home, tears rolling down his cheeks as I stood beside him. It was like a death watch. I expressed my sorrow. He said he was losing his Hawaiian lifestyle anyway. He had seen what we call progress (development) disregard the people—his family picnic grounds dominated by unfriendly strangers, fish ponds polluted by cesspools. The people of Kalapana have opened my eyes. They made me change my priorities as a government official."

Kim believes that visitors as well as government officials should respect local traditions and try to understand the feelings of native people.

Harry Kim, Hawai'i County Civil Defense director.

CHAPTER SIX

THE POWER OF PELE

An echo of the controversy that once raged between *kāhuna* and missionaries about the fire goddess has erupted again over a new technology in volcano country, geothermal power. Once more, adherents of different beliefs have confronted one another concerning the power of Pele and how it should affect our lives. The dispute, centered in once-remote Puna, is a complicated one and important for our time.

For several decades, thoughtful residents have been concerned about Hawai'i's dependence on imported fuel oil; the islands have no oil wells or coal mines. This concern has resulted in many attempts to develop alternative energy sources, including solar panels and windmills. The use of bagasse, or dried sugar cane refuse, as fuel to run sugar mills has increased dramatically. Successful experiments with ocean thermal energy conversion have produced a new if small source of clean power.

The alternate energy source that appears to have the greatest potential to produce sizable amounts of power in Hawai'i is geothermal energy, the power of Pele, usable energy contained in underground steam. For years it was only potential. A headline on October 9, 1968, read, "Volcanic Steam Studied in Hawaii." The story explained that a company planned to drill experimental wells at the volcano, thus eliminating some of the need to ship oil in tankers to Hawai'i.

Politicians hailed the idea, but several scientists criticized it. They pointed out that as early as the 1950s, two companies made test borings in Puna but found only low-pressure, low-temperature steam. Yet geothermal wells in New Zealand, Italy and Mexico were producing electricity. And geothermal enthusiasts asserted that volcano energy was cleaner than oil or coal.

But these arguments continued to produce little more than rhetorical energy. In 1973 another drill rig went up near Kīlauea Volcano. A Colorado geophysicist drilled more than half a mile without finding enough heat to boil water. Still the dream survived, and a new consortium, after an 18-month

Geothermal drill rig in Wao Kele O Puna rain forest - Puna, Hawai'i.

survey of Puna, concluded in 1974 that geothermal energy there could indeed provide a viable alternative to oil.

Politicians and scientists gathered at Pohoiki in Puna on November 23, 1975, to witness the start of a $1 million gamble as drilling began for still another well. This time drillers found steam more than hot enough to produce electricity. A flash test of four hours proved successful in 1976 and the promoters of geothermal energy went, if you will pardon the expression, full steam ahead.

Problems immediately arose. Sulphur fumes from the well made residents fume as well. They cited health hazards, but local health officials concluded that tests did not bear out these claims. A small geothermal power plant, financed by government funds, including some from the federal government, began producing power for commercial sale. Now Hawaiian activists jumped into the dispute, maintaining that the power underground belonged not to commercial companies but to Pele.

This complication over native rights threatened to kill federal funds. The dispute headed for the courts while local residents lined up on both sides. It was not a Hawaiian versus *haole* (foreigner) dispute; some Hawaiians, such as Puna landowner Richard Lyman, lauded geothermal energy as a wave of the future. The Big Island County Council approved drilling of another, private well with $1.5 million at stake.

Prospects seemed so bright that in 1980 the Bishop Estate, Hawaiʻi's

largest private landowner, asked the circuit court for permission to develop some of its Puna acreage as a geothermal energy field. Other developers jumped into the competition. There was already talk of an undersea cable that would carry electrical power from Hawaiʻi to Oʻahu. Meanwhile, protesters carried signs calling for agriculture instead of geothermal energy development in Puna.

The dispute entered a new phase when another large landowner,

Left, *Blowout well.*

Right, *Geothermal development (Ormat) in residential Puna.*

Anti-geothermal protesters - Hilo, Hawai'i.

the Campbell Estate, asked approval from the Land Board to drill 35 test wells on acreage adjoining the Hawai'i Volcanoes National Park. This time the protesters had a new ally. The National Park Service opposed the placing of an industrial project so near a park dedicated to the preservation of rare flora and fauna.

Yet trustees of the Office of Hawaiian Affairs, a state department established to improve the lot of native Hawaiians, voted to back the Campbell Estate proposal. And the estate received limited rights to drill experimentally near the park. In addition, a federal judge turned down a request from Hawaiian activists for an injunction to stop geothermal energy production in Puna.

Then Pele seemed to take matters into her own hands. The 1983 eruption began, sending lava flows that eventually covered half of Campbell Estate's geothermal reservation. Heartened, foes of geothermal renewed their protests. They won a small victory when Campbell Estate abandoned original plans. But they lost the battle when the estate exchanged its lands near the park for state land in Puna. Drilling went ahead, and a third well proved successful.

Still, opposition to the geothermal industry kept growing. A group called the Pele Defense Fund took the issue of native Hawaiian rights to the State Supreme Court, arguing that geothermal drilling violated the sanctity of the Hawaiian goddess they worshiped. In 1987 the court ruled that the project did not threaten Pele worship. So the Pele Defense Fund placed full-page ads in U.S. mainland newspapers to state its case. Officials of the Hawai'i Visitors Bureau expressed concern that the ads would hurt tourism. Pele worshipers lost again when the Supreme Court of the United States ruled against them in 1988.

A Hawaiian protests at Wao Kele O Puna Rain Forest by chaining himself to gate.

By this time, many people in Hawai'i had chosen sides in the issue and, in 1989, the Rain Forest Action Group based in Berkeley, California joined the opposition to geothermal drilling in Puna. Protests resulted first in five arrests, then 39 more. At about the same time, plans for a $450 million power transmission cable from the Big Island to O'ahu went ahead, and the Hawaiian Electric Company in Honolulu agreed to invest in geothermal power.

Until this time, opposition to geothermal as an alternate source of energy had come from residents who objected to noise and fumes from the neighborhood geothermal power plant, from people who complained of ailments they said were caused by the fumes, and from those Hawaiians who believed the drilling to be a desecration of Pele.

In 1990 a new objection arose. Environmentalists around the world discovered that geothermal drilling in Puna could threaten the rare and fragile tropical rain forest there. The Sierra Club Legal Defense Fund filed suit to stop the drilling, and protesters increased in numbers. One demonstration resulted in 132 arrests.

At this writing, the weight of government and industry in Hawai'i is in favor of developing Hawai'i's geothermal potential as a viable alternative to dangerous dependence on oil. If geothermal is not entirely "clean," supporters argue, it is cleaner than the alternatives, and new technology will eliminate noise and fumes. Major companies continue plans to utilize and profit from geothermal energy as a means to help maintain Hawai'i's standard of living in a responsible way into the 21st century.

Their ultimate goal is 20 geothermal power plants in sleepy Puna, each with eight to 10 wells, in addition to the laying of power cables.

The active opposition argues that, before plunging into geothermal development, Hawai'i should use energy conservation to reduce its dependence on imported fuel. They contend that geothermal is "dirtier" than the public realizes, and that even limited invasion of the rain forest by geothermal developers will introduce exotic plants that must eventually destroy the pristine rain forest environment. In response, both state and county governments have imposed more stringent requirements on geothermal developers.

"Blowouts," or the uncontrolled release of superheated steam while wells were being drilled, created renewed opposition because of the noise, offensive smell and a health hazard now acknowledged by experts. Residents living near the geothermal field had to be evacuated during a major blowout in 1991. Government enthusiasm for geothermal drilling cooled with a realization that the volcano country of Puna is a unique place, and that the technology for drilling into a live volcano may not be as reliably safe as first supposed.

The above is merely an outline of the basic arguments; new complications continue to arise. So the power of Pele is still in dispute. The volcano country remains an important place in terms of human values that mean different things to different people. You will have to decide for yourself.

Children play at Wao Kele O Puna Rain Forest.

CHAPTER SEVEN

HOW TO EXPLORE THE VOLCANO

One early visitor who failed to appreciate volcano country was Mark Twain. But he had a good excuse. He was nearing the end of a horseback ride around the Big Island and, by the time he finished, he was so saddle sore he ended up in bed. His mistake, one that people still make, was in trying to cover too much ground too fast.

The best way to enjoy the volcano is to give yourself a little time, at least two days. Wear clothes you would for hiking, and bring something warm enough for the night chill at higher altitudes. A dependable flashlight is good to have in case you get a chance to view an eruption at night.

Volcano country is easily accessible. Hawai'i Volcanoes National Park and Puna are both less than an hour by car from the hotels in Hilo. There are also places to stay at the volcano. Hotels on the other side of the island on the Kona Coast are about three hours away.

Here are some suggestions for exploring volcano country. You will need a road map of the island, as well as the maps for trails and roads available at park headquarters.

Drives

Crater Rim Road—The first thing most people do after entering the park is drive the Crater Rim Road, which begins near the entrance. Brochures that contain maps are available at the entrance or at park headquarters. The Crater Rim Road leads around the caldera of Kīlauea. Signs direct you to points of

Tourists watch lava enter the Pacific Ocean. (Hawai'i Volcanoes National Park, Hawai'i)

interest along the way. You can zip around in half an hour or spend all morning. There's enough to see.

Chain of Craters Road—A park highway leads down from Kīlauea to sea level, past old craters and many lava flows, through forest and into raw lava, where drivers must turn back. Here you will see what you have read about in Chapters One and Three. The road leads to points where the recent eruption flows into the sea.

Hilina Pali Road—For people with enough time, this road is a delightful drive, leading off from the Chain of Craters Road, through dry and picturesque volcano wilderness on the border of the Ka'ū Desert. The road ends at an overlook where foot trails lead down a *pali* or cliff. The view of the seacoast is awesome.

Mauna Loa Strip Road—Instead of going down to the sea, this road climbs upward from Kīlauea Crater on the broad slope of Mauna Loa to about 6600 feet into grassland and *koa* forest. You will pass Kipuka Puaulu Bird Park, and there are birds among the *koa* trees there. This is a morning or afternoon drive.

Puna Coast Road—On the highway that connects Hilo and the volcano, you turn toward the sea at Keaau. Continue on broad pavement to the turnoff to Kapoho. The road leads to the sea past Lava Tree Park and emerges among the lava flows of the Kapoho eruption. Turn right along the tropical coast on a narrow, winding road through marvelous, mysterious Puna, a Hawai'i visitors seldom see. At 'Opihikao Church a sign will point you back to the main road.

Now let's return to the Hawai'i Volcanoes National Park.

Points of Interest

Visitor's Center—This is a good place to start your adventure after you arrive at the volcano. Here you can pick up maps and ask for information. There is a small museum and a bookstore where you can buy most of the reading material recommended in the preceding chapters. Park rangers are on hand to answer questions.

Volcano Art Center—Located a few steps from Visitor's Center, this gallery is housed in the original Volcano House built in 1877, an interesting and historic structure. Here you will find handicrafts and art objects of first quality, and people who can tell you about the artists.

Thomas A. Jaggar Museum—You will find here a grand view of Kīlauea Crater and the firepit of Halema'uma'u, the home of Pele. Inside is the delightful Jaggar Museum with displays of the geology and mythology of Hawaiian volcanoes that appeal to children as well as adults. You will also find a small bookstore. The observatory where volcanologists work is next door.

Hawai'i Volcanoes National Park.

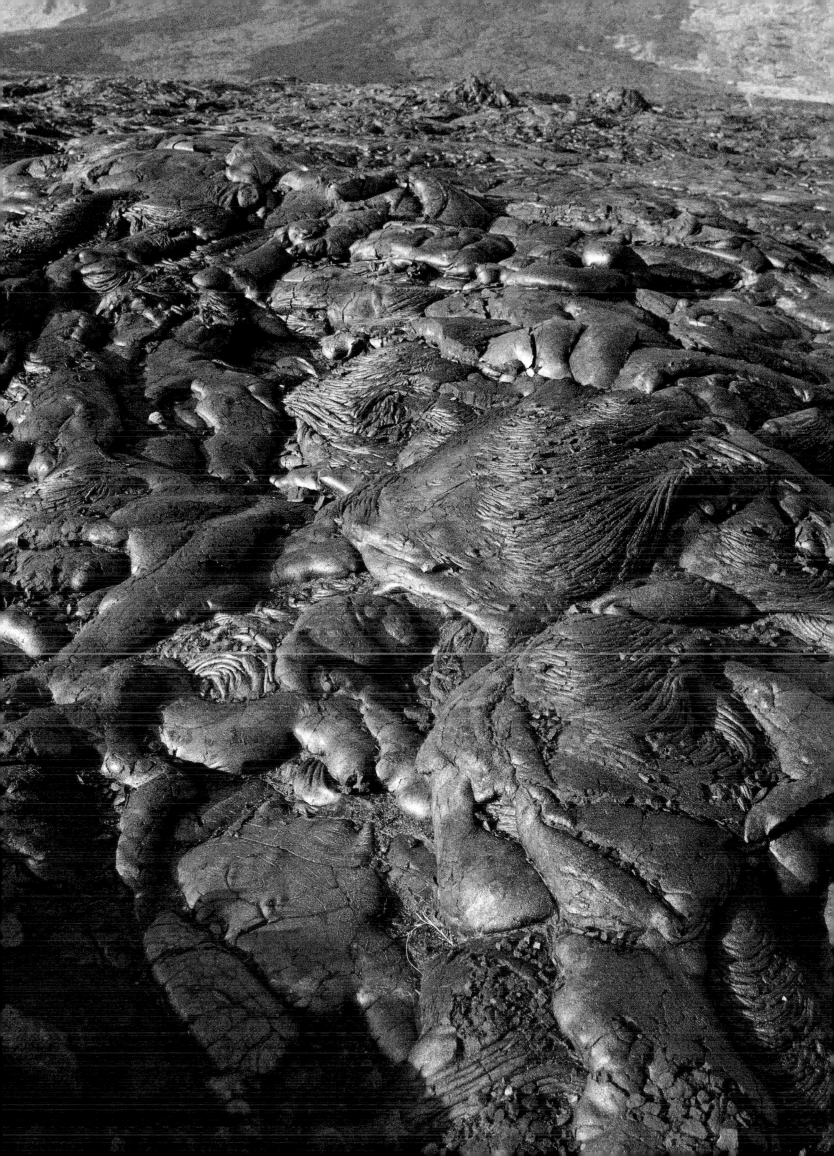

Petroglyph game board - Puna, Hawai'i.

Thurston Lava Tube— This popular stop along the Crater Rim Road is located in a magnificent fern forest. An easy paved trail leads into the dark lava tube, lighted now for your safety.

Pu'uloa Petroglyphs— Watch for the sign along the Chain of Craters Road as you near the sea. A rough foot trail half a mile long leads to the petroglyphs. The park does not indicate the petroglyphs on a map because some people, not realizing how fragile and historic the petroglyphs are, destroy them. Don't deface these treasures of prehistoric art.

Kamoamoa Campground—What was once an ancient Hawaiian village by the sea has been partially covered by black sand. Please don't disturb the ruins. This is a fine place to picnic and to view the unusual coastline at close range. The campground, with toilets, is located on the Chain of Craters Road as you drive along the shore.

Hikes

Steam Vent Walk—A delightful and easy introduction to Pele's domain, this hike begins at the Visitor's Center parking lot. The trail leads to the rim of Kīlauea Crater, where steam rises from cracks in the lava, most visible in early morning. You will pass the Sulphur Banks, steam vents on the trail and a forest of yellow ginger, then emerge at the parking lot.

Kīlauea Iki Trail—This is my favorite walk at the volcano because the trail leads through tropical rain forest, past view after spectacular view, among rare birds, and across the grim floor of a steaming volcano crater. Plan on about two hours. It's 3.4 miles and good exercise. Start at the Thurston Lava Tube parking lot and walk counterclockwise.

Devastation Trail—Here is another easy walk where the creative as well as the destructive dimensions of the volcano are on display. A boardwalk starting near the parking lot leads across a desert of ash where gray skeletons of dead trees stand in silent testimony to the destructive power of Pele. Yet this desert is already green with new life. You may veer left instead of taking the boardwalk. Watch for a 35 mph speed limit sign that pokes through the ashes. Follow a footworn path over the cinders to high ground for an exceptional view of three volcanoes: Kīlauea, Mauna Loa and Mauna Kea. Look for ʻōhelo bushes.

View of Kīlauea Iki.

Lava Tree Walk—You won't find a Lava Tree Walk listed on the maps, so follow these directions. About one-quarter of a mile from the start of the Chain of Craters Road, you will see a trail crossing. Park your car and take the trail on the right. An easy 15 minutes of pleasant walking will take you through rain forest and then out on new lava. Look to your left for arches in black stone. Go to them and look around. You will see the contorted shapes of lava trees all round you.

Fern Forest Walk—Instead of going to the right at the trail crossing near the start of Chain of Craters Road, take the trail that leads off to the left. It goes to the Thurston Lava Tube and through a jungle of ferns that tower over your head.

There are many more and longer trails for overnight hikers. Maps of these trails are available at the Visitor's Center. If you plan an overnight hike, the park requires you to check in first for your own safety.

Lush ferns make up jungle scene.

69

CHAPTER EIGHT

THE VOLCANOES OF MAUI, KAUA'I, O'AHU, MOLOKA'I, AND LĀNA'I

Volcano hunting on Maui, Kaua'i, O'ahu, Moloka'i and Lāna'i is more elusive than on the Island of Hawai'i because the lava fountains long ago turned to cold stone, and the smoothly rounded domes of the oldest islands have been eroded in maturity into picturesque valleys and craggy mountains.

An understanding of this fascinating process of nature can add a great deal of interest to your visit, and will allow you to appreciate more fully the grand sweep of island formation that never stops.

Remember, wherever you are in Hawai'i, your foot falls on a volcano. Each volcano is different, and exploring any—or many—of them is a marvelous adventure. Here is some advice on how to do it and what to look for on the older volcanic islands. Let's begin with Maui.

A magnificent view of Kalalau Valley Overlook, Kaua'i.

Haleakalā on Maui

Maui is made up of two volcanic mountains, Haleakalā and East Maui, that joined to form the island. Of the two, Haleakalā is better known, second only to the volcanoes of the Big Island as a visitor attraction.

Haleakalā, or House of the Sun, towers in lofty splendor above the many scenic marvels that have caused residents of the island to adopt the slogan, "Maui No Ka Oe"—"Maui Is The Best." The tawny summit of the volcano, sometimes capped with snow, often stands clear against the blue Hawaiian sky in the morning. Afternoon clouds usually cloak the broad shoulders of Haleakalā in a shroud of gray.

Haleakalā is very different from volcano country on the Big Island. A drive to the summit is a little like leaving earth for outer space. Your launching pad, however, is not Cape Kennedy but the tropical island of Maui. You will likely leave from a resort at Kāʻanapali or a hotel in the old whaling town of Lahaina, and drive by miles of beach and palm trees before climbing gently into fields of tall sugar cane.

The highway rises and curves into cool meadowland under stands of shaggy eucalyptus trees, then twists and winds upward past the rain belt through clumps of dry grass growing on rough lava. The tropical shore is far behind now, and the clouds hang close overhead. Most likely you will drive through them, up and up, climbing into space.

Above the clouds you enter a different world of harsh, cold lava desert, a scene of sterile ash and rock and life forms that have adapted to this environment. The strange, cactus-like plant you see is the silversword. It is endemic to this frigid moonscape. Some varieties grow on the Big Island.

By the time you reach the summit, you will have climbed to 10,023 feet. In this rarefied atmosphere, a community of scientists staffs the round, white observatories perched on cold cinder cones, testing laser beams and conducting other experiments.

Here is a stirring view of the House of the Sun, a giant volcano crater big enough to swallow Manhattan, a sweep of high-altitude silence dotted by cinder cones as big as Diamond Head but miniature from this commanding height of more than 1000 feet. Haleakalā Crater is a still life of muted fire colors: burnt red, gray, purple, rusty orange, black and sulphur yellow. For old Hawaiians, the crater was a mystical place. For people of the space age, it is also a grand adventure.

Birth of Haleakalā

This sleeping giant that forms the eastern part of Maui is not, in scientific terms, extinct. It is merely dormant. It last erupted in about 1790. Its age has been estimated at between 690,000 and 830,000 years. Like other Hawaiian shield volcanoes, it was formed by the piling of one lava flow upon another.

Sliding Sands Trail - Haleakalā National Park.

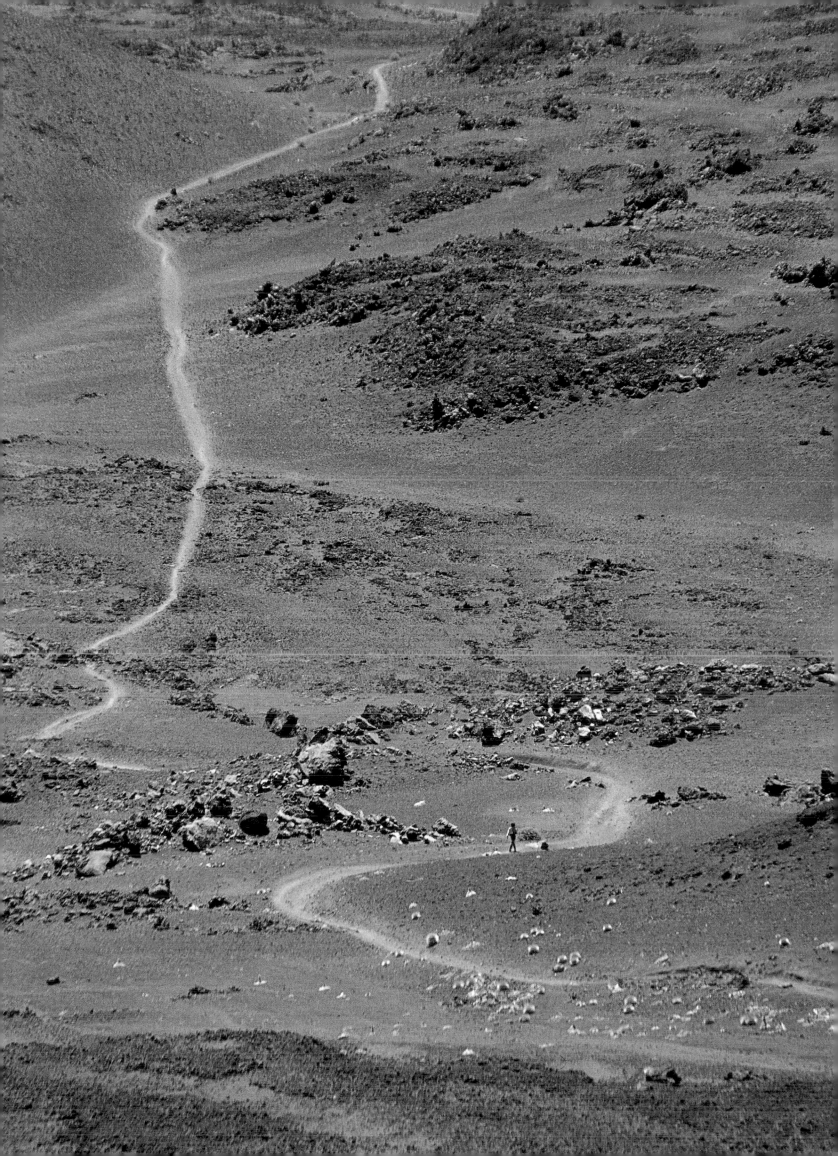

The formation of the vast crater is a more interesting story, according to geologists. As eruptions lost their vitality, erosion by water began, cutting away the smooth surface to create an enormous amphitheater even while the vents still spewed lava and ash. For hundreds of thousands of years, fire and water battled to create this place.

Water outlasted fire, and erosion continued to form the crater. But fire returned in one last burst of energy to build the picturesque cinder cones that give Haleakalā Crater its volcanic signature. And so you see in a magnificent panorama the result of elemental conflict. Yet here Pele met her match. Haleakalā Crater is primarily erosional in origin.

Mythology of Haleakalā

Ancient Hawaiians, with their sophisticated understanding of volcanology, related in their chants that Pele did not choose Haleakalā as a home. Instead, she went on to Kīlauea, still giving birth to the islands by fire. For this reason, the hero of Haleakalā is a different figure in the Hawaiian pantheon of gods and demigods.

He is the demigod Māui, known throughout Polynesia as a rascal, an imp, a jokester who was always playing tricks. He, too, is credited with creating islands—by bringing them up from the sea with his magic fishhook. Māui was very popular because he was adept at dreaming up novel technology that made life easier.

The great myth of Haleakalā concerns the sun. It appears that, in ancient times, the sun traveled too rapidly across the sky for Māui's mother to dry her laundry. Māui, the imaginative imp, pondered the problem and reached a solution. One morning he lassoed the sun's rays and forced this irresponsible lord of the sky to travel more slowly in the heavens for the benefit of humans below. So the volcano is known as the House of the Sun.

A sunrise on the rim of Haleakalā continues to be a spectacular experience. People still get out of bed in the dark to drive up and see it.

Crater Bound Outfitters. Haleakalā Crater, Maui.

Points of Interest

Hosmer Grove—At 6800 feet on the smooth road to the summit of Haleakalā is a sign for and turnoff to Hosmer Grove, a natural botanical park that offers glimpses into the plant life of Maui volcano country. An easy half-mile trail over pine needles and through forest is posted with little signs telling what rare plants, as well as familiar ones, you are seeing: spicy juniper, cypress, fir, spruce, native sandalwood, *'ohi'a*, *mamane*, *'ōhelo* and *pukiawe*.

Ranger Station—A little way beyond Hosmer Grove is the headquarters of Haleakalā National Park, where you check in for hikes in the crater and get information about the park. Here are nature displays and a small bookstore with informative publications about this fascinating place.

Summit Lookout—As you near the summit, watch for signs that point to places where you can view the crater. The most impressive is at the summit itself. Here you will find a shelter, protected from the wind, that has nature displays and a large model of the mountain and crater.

Hikes

Trails lead through the crater to three overnight cabins. These cabins are so popular that reservations are required ahead of time. To walk amid such pristine lava wilderness is an adventure that people who love nature find inspiring. You can get a taste of it at the summit by walking for a way down the Sliding Sands Trail that leads off from the lookout. But beware of going too far. Climbing back at 10,000 feet can strain your heart and lungs.

Tips for Exploring Haleakalā

The drive up the mountain is easy because your auto or tour bus does the work. You will enjoy the view more if you bring a jacket because it's cold on the rim, and you will want to spend some time in comfort as you contemplate the vast panorama of Haleakalā. Hikes into the crater are for people conditioned to exercise. If you are up to it, don't miss the opportunity.

Holua cabin - Haleakalā Crater, Maui.

Kaua'i

This lush, tropical island is a single volcano 5170 feet high, 72 miles northwest of O'ahu, roughly circular in shape, a dome of basalt that has been sculpted by the elements into fanciful shapes. Though only 33 miles long and 25 miles wide, Kaua'i is a scenic wonderland. All of it has been created by forces of nature from volcanic raw materials. The

Waimea Canyon - Kaua'i.

Kaua'i volcano built a crater 13 miles across. It is unrecognizable now except to geologists, for erosion has transformed it into a summit plateau.

The whimsy of nature added another unlikely touch, a high-altitude swamp wrapped in mist and mystery. The Alaka'i Swamp is on top of Kaua'i because this is one of the wettest spots on earth. Fifty feet of rain falls here every year, and it has to run off somewhere. So it flows in streams in all directions. Over the eons these streams have cut spectacular valleys into the original bald dome of Kaua'i.

Guidebooks declare Waimea Canyon the most spectacular on Kaua'i, but that is only because it is the most accessible. This canyon is 14 1/2 miles long and 2700 feet deep, and is easily reachable by highway. A paved road winds up past impressive vistas of cliffs reminiscent of the Great Southwest.

At the forested level of the Alaka'i Swamp, hiking trails lead away to remote and fascinating places, including the swamp and the canyon. The starting place for these adventures is located at about 4000 feet. There you will find a State Park headquarters; the Koke'e Lodge, which has a restaurant and shop; cabins for rent, and the rustic Koke'e Museum, with its displays on the wildlife inhabiting Koke'e and bookstore stocked with maps and literature about the area.

Friends who own a cabin in Koke'e tell me the area has hundreds of miles of hiking trails, the best in the state, leading out from this central point. On the road that continues from the lodge to the Kalalau Valley lookouts, signs point to more trails that follow the crater rim and lead into the canyon.

The lookouts over Kalalau Valley on Kaua'i's north shore provide sweeping vistas and revealing insights into how this island developed from its volcanic origins. One method employed by nature for such gigantic sculpting is called "mass wasting." A spectacular demonstration of mass wasting occurred in 1981 when part of the mountain face in nearby Olokele Canyon tore away in a free fall, then rumbled two-thirds of a mile along the floor of the canyon. The landslide was caused by high rainfall and underground water seepage.

This northern side of Kaua'i is called the Nāpali (cliff) Coast, and the cliffs facing the ocean are evidence of the complicated forces constantly at work to change the shape of volcanic islands.

One force that forms sea cliffs is called "marine erosion." The northeast trade winds today drive waves against the Nāpali cliffs as they once drove them against the sloping base of the young volcano. Waves hurled sand and rock against the shore, cutting it away to form a terrace, then a low sea cliff. The cutting continued, digging "nips" at the base of the cliff and causing the cliff above to give way. Eventually sea cliffs reached the towering heights seen on the Nāpali Coast.

Another force that changes the shape of volcanic islands is stream erosion. You will find more about that in the section on Moloka'i.

The trails of Koke'e lead to many overlooks with views of valleys and canyons. One word of caution: the trail that leads into the Alaka'i Swamp from the last Kalalau lookout is well marked and provides easy walking for only a mile or two. Then the trail enters bogs, and hikers can easily get lost. This place is for strong hikers only and for no one alone.

O'ahu

Hawai'i's capital island, O'ahu, was formed by two volcanoes. What is left of them are the Wai'anae and Ko'olau Mountain Ranges. Gradually, after the domes of the volcanoes broke the surface of the ocean, they enlarged and merged to form a single island. Neither of the original domes is recognizable now as a typical Hawaiian shield volcano.

Eruption ceased at last, only to break out again to form craters that remain distinctly volcanic in appearance. These are the craters of Diamond Head, Punchbowl and Koko Head. Each offers its own unique history.

The inside of Punchbowl Crater has become the National Cemetery of the Pacific, a shrine to U.S. war dead and the most visited place in Hawai'i. There is also an impressive view of Honolulu from the lookout.

Diamond Head Crater is accessible via a paved road that leads through a tunnel carved into the crater side to a National Guard base inside. A popular trail leads from a parking area, with rest rooms, across the crater floor and twists up to the rim. There you have sweeping views of Waikīkī and downtown Honolulu, and the entire coastline on either side. Try to bring a flashlight, as the trail's tunnel is dark.

At Koko Head, beyond Diamond Head, one side of the crater collapsed to let in the ocean and create what is now an underwater park called Hanauma Bay. Fish feed on the reefs that formed in the shallow bay. Because the area is now off limits to fishermen, the fish have multiplied so that you are eyeball-to-eyeball with many species as you paddle along with your snorkel. The place is so popular that parking spaces are hard to find.

Nāpali Coast, Kaua'i.

Moloka'i

Like O'ahu, Moloka'i was formed by two volcanoes, those of East and West Moloka'i. They joined to build an island that today is 38 miles long and 10 miles wide across the channel and southeast of O'ahu. Moloka'i was once part of a gigantic island that submerged. The mountain tops formed smaller islands that include Maui, Lāna'i and Kaho'olawe as well as Moloka'i. The climatic and scenic variations on this small volcanic island, as on all of the Hawaiian Islands, are dramatic.

One of Moloka'i's most impressive features is a cliff coastline on the northeast side where nature has carved tropical valleys, uninhabited now except for campers, similar to those on the Nāpali Coast. You may fly by on your way to Maui or Hawai'i. If you do, don't miss the opportunity to study this amazing example of how streams and waterfalls exert their will upon volcanic stone.

The deep valleys began with stream erosion that cut V-shaped notches into the land surface, primarily during times of flooding. Landslides that fall away from the steep sides of the notches widen the valley as the stream cuts deeper and deeper.

Not all streams cut valleys, because to do so requires a certain combination of soil composition and climatic condition. But stream erosion is a common cause of valley formation in Hawai'i's volcanic islands.

Waterfalls are also effective as sculptors' chisels. Watch a waterfall as it plunges down the face of a Moloka'i cliff. See how it cuts a groove. The next time you glance at a volcanic mountain range on O'ahu or Kaua'i, notice the flutes in the mountain ridges. They were carved by waterfalls, one of many tools in nature's island-forming tool chest.

Lāna'i

Third smallest of the major Hawaiian Islands, Lāna'i is a single volcano 3370 feet high. It lies in clear sight from Maui and Moloka'i, is about 13 miles across and has only recently begun to be developed as a major resort. The former caldera of Lāna'i is called Pālāwai Basin, four miles long and three miles wide, but difficult for all but experts to recognize.

The marine cliffs on Lāna'i are on the southwest side, not the northeast. The cold lava of these cliffs tells a fascinating story. High in the cliffs are marine fossils. They were deposited there, like a ring of dirt around a bathtub, by a giant tidal wave created when the entire southwestern side of Mauna Loa slid into the ocean. The marine fossils of Lāna'i are more than 1000 feet above sea level, believed the highest ever found in the Central Pacific.

Catamaran on Waikīkī Beach, O'ahu.

Lava entering ocean - Kalapana, Hawai'i.

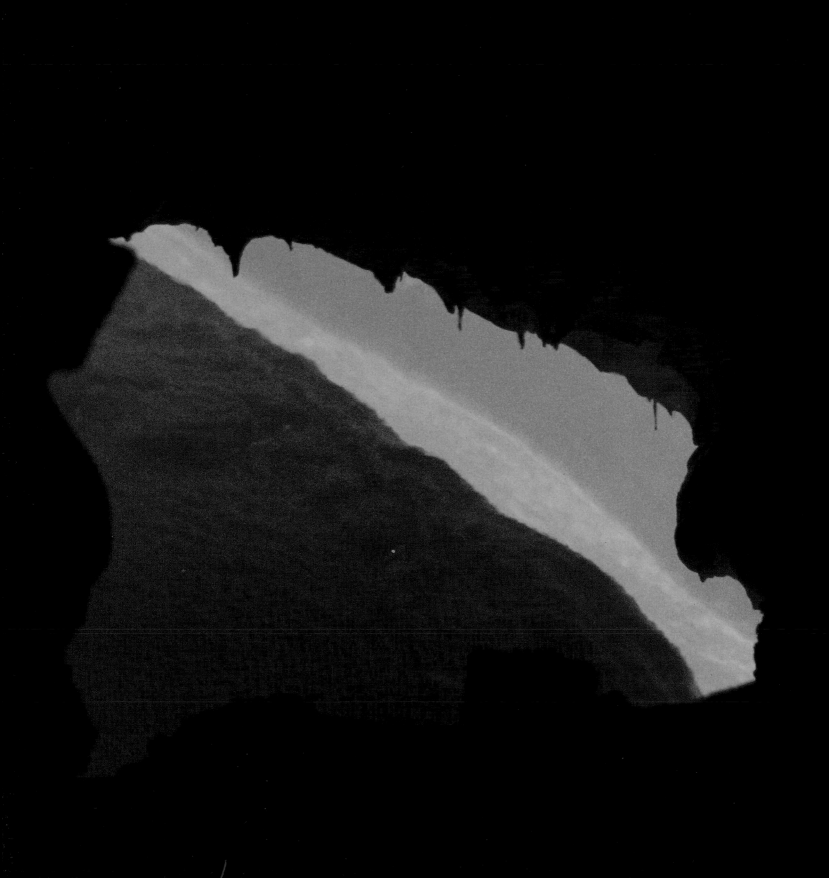

About This Book

Remember, this book is meant to be only an introduction to the adventures you can find among the volcanoes of the Hawaiian Islands. Don't hesitate to read more, to explore, to ask questions. There is no place in the world where the answers are more readily available. Good hunting.

Lava tube at Kīlauea Volcano.

INDEX

Lava flow at Kīlauea Volcano by moonlight.

Kalapana Mist.

Birth by Fire
A Guide to Hawai'i's Volcanoes

Written by Bob Krauss
Photographs by G. Brad Lewis
Book Design by Terry Nii, Eric Woo Design

Copyright ©1992 Island Heritage Publishing
First Edition, First Printing – 1992
ISBN Number: 0-89610-228-9

Address orders and correspondence to:

 ISLAND HERITAGE PUBLISHING

A division of The Madden Corporation
99-880 Iwaena Street
Aiea, Hawaii 96701
(808) 487-7299